IN WHOM IS MY

DELIGHT

POEMS BY

Tad Cornell

Juggling Teacups Press

Philadelphia, PA

ISBN: 978-0-9908633-0-4

"A Second Childhood" first published in
The Ballad of St. Barbara and Other Verses
by Gilbert Keith Chesterton, London: Cecil Palmer, 1922.

Cover image is a detail of a painting
"Christ Among the Doctors" by Bernardino Luini

tadcornell6331@gmail.com

tadcornell.com

Juggling Teacups Press

Philadelphia, PA

Behold, the crowning mercies melt,

The first surprises stay;

And in my dross is dropped a gift

For which I dare not pray:

That a man grow used to grief and joy

But not to night and day.

~ G. K. Chesterton, from "A Second Childhood"

CONTENTS

SPECTACULUM

And deeper than did ever plummet sound
I'll drown my book!
~Prospero in *The Tempest*

SPECTACULUM I

Spectaculum facti sumus Deo, angelis et hominibus . . .

Having drowned my book,
     and so conspicuously
before God and angels and
     passers-by who could care less,
now it's back to haunt me.

The grisly death of Father Edmund,
     drawn and quartered, they say
was all in a day's tedium
     compared with the antics
of the Two Dutchmen that day.

One, a midget with stumps
     for arms who held the floor
juggling teacups, the other a giant!
     Even less of public note,
my book, become a floating door.

Tad Cornell

One could hope, this Feast of
    Thomas, should its hinges
swing wide, this door might feature
    the Two Dutchmen
and not this poet's famous binges.

The door being soggy, and I now
    all wet, my story either sane
or a pitiless farce, these fingers when
    pressed where nails had been
will unlock my last will to complain.

SPECTACULUM II

In Hoc Signo Vinces: Asceterium

In the flooding, the door had washed
        downstream cheek to cheek
with garbage bags and lawn chairs.
        I had put on my hip boots
and had dragged it across the creek.

I dragged it to the closer bank,
        out of my sight because I could.
But that first night I heard a voice:
        "In all thy works, keep pre-eminence!"
Thus spake my embanked wood.

That morning, Independence Day,
        when our homes should be brave and free,
that door kept quoting Ecclesiasticus:
        "As long as thou livest, and hast
breath in thee, let no man change thee."

Tad Cornell

"Give not to son or wife,

   brother or friend, control

over thee while thou livest,

   and give not thy estate

to another . . ." It troubled my soul.

I feared if I turned the door's knob

   it might become, again, my book.

Instead it swung open to another world

   within a town called Nazareth.

I stepped inside to take a look.

SPECTACULUM III

Digitus Dei est hic.

It seemed like a dream. Laughter,
     and singing as the shops closed:
"Those who are sowing in tears
     will sing when they reap." Little mother:
"What marvels," as her baby dozed.

"See, I place my words in your mouth!"
     Yosef, the leader, so they implied,
proclaimed this oddity which all affirmed.
     "We who build for man's shelter,
tonight do honor bridegroom and bride!"

A shudder, maybe of landing, or the dread
     that a nuptial feast was code
for the last scroll rolled, I don't know . . .
     I became a servant of the wedding.
I was vigilant in angelic mode.

While outside the deer emerged
          to lap from the mountain stream,
the moon was also poised to swing
          from the Compestella rafters of
a cloud-bursting sky in this Nazareth dream.

Upon Yosef's roof, the rain
          punctuated a serenity that grew
that night. The bride favored me
          with her trust in a crucial errand!
I was servant to the working crew!

SPECTACULUM IV

. . . ex quo nobis fiet panis vitae.

In candle light glimmerings
      the night danced in his eyes
which always, it seemed, were on me.
      He was younger than twelve.
The guests asked him to rise.

Yehoshua, son of Yosef
      sang for them. They wept.
His voice was pure and sweet
      in praise of the Juniper tree
under which Elijah had slept.

Its slender leaves so useful
      making brooms, its bloom
cascading daffodil trumpets
      to announce God's angel
and fill Jerusalem's womb.

When he sang of Elijah's prayer
      for death, he looked at me.
His mission failed, a wasted life
      with only sleep to console him.
The end of life was not to be.

Startled awake, and twice they say,
      the angel ordered him: "Eat!"
Hearth cake manna and water at his head,
      the one who would be dead
now walks on glory's feet.

SPECTACULUM V

Finitum capax infiniti

His mother, it must have been,
        whispered with radiant face
into his left ear when he sat
        to a stunned, awed response
until applause possessed the place.

And as the clamor grew, the boy
        just listened, sober, rapt
to all his mother had to say.
        And it was this tableau that fixed
itself in my mind, a bird that is trapped.

The next day dawned after fitful sleep
        to routine bodily functions blessed
by my hearing, as I met these needs,
        the songs of praise to God by all
but me under Yosef's roof. A test

was being hatched. Can the body
          ever know the Ghost Sublime?
My body cried a yes amid
          disgraceful vulgate, burdens freed
like Purgatory at the end of time.

And then I saw him in the light of day.
          He was serving from his mother's pan
the morning cake to sustain the workers
          soon to travel to the camp,
the construction site, to build as man can.

SPECTACULUM VI

Quoniam sine dominico non possumus.

"And your morning sacrifice?" He smiled
      warmly at my perplexity.
"Now, now, Yehoshua," his mother said,
      "our guest is hungry," as the men
bustled out the door. A silent plea

was hammering from inside my chest,
      and the boy crossed the room
and took my hand and led me outside
      and gestured wide and beaming
to the placid sky and earthly bloom.

When he closed his eyes, I closed mine.
      I witnessed then and there a man,
owner of a house in North Africa,
      responding to an imperial proconsul
who was making this repeated demand:

"Why did you permit entry through your door
        a gathering of those who insist
on celebrating this forbidden Rite of Thanks?"
        "I could not do otherwise," he said.
"Without what is the Lord's, we cannot exist."

Delight saturated my mind. I opened my eyes.
        The boy's mother, Miriam by name,
was calling us inside to eat. And he made
        as if to race me to the table, so we lunged,
laughing. Somehow I felt free of all blame.

SPECTACULUM VII

Summae Deus clementiae . . .

Breakfast consumed, this son of Yosef
       gestured, and I followed out
into the compound that was Nazareth,
       extended family dwellings round
a courtyard. I began to doubt.

How can this squalid place teach me
       why my book should not be drowned?
In all this farmyard stench, wisdom?
       And then the workshop entered me
more truly than I entered it, like sound.

Music was the craft that Nazareth hid.
       The *nevel,* a twelve-stringed harp,
kinnor, the lyre of ten strings favored
       by David, *halil,* a large flute, *tof,*
a small drum, and tools refined and sharp.

And the room was filled with women at work,
      their children helping, to craft in wood
these instruments of worship to sell,
      to synagogues for weddings and feast days,
and to the Jerusalem Temple if they could.

I watched as Yehoshua and his mother
      labored to hollow out a ram's horn
to make the trumpet called *shofar*.
      My job was to sing a baby to sleep,
my chest to be chamber for the not yet born.

SPECTACULUM VIII

Virum non cognosco.

My thumping heart counts in tiny ears . . .
     in persona matris to this child
that Miriam had put into my arms,
     one of hers, I thought . . . Yehoshua
stopped his work, turned, and smiled.

He spoke into my mind these words:
     "My mother has never known man."
He turned back, leaving me confused.
     A late morning pause in laboring
brought for me a welcome change in plan.

The real mother reclaimed her baby
     as all gathered round to sing a psalm:
"*As a child has rest in his mother's arms,*
     even so my soul." A curious choice.
Miriam then spoke with earnestness and calm

of how there was once a king with twin girls
       named Avotha and Shamar. When asked,
the children said the first meant "to serve,"
       and the second meant "to guard."
These royal daughters were given a task.

A serpent will come into this kingdom.
       Our salvation is the life inside your names.
If you find that life in time, the evil dies.
       They found the life! Where? Server
guarded Guard, Guard served serpent flames!

SPECTACULUM IX

Beati mundo corde.

A distant shofar blast now thrilled
      the room. Kinfolk from Bethany!
"Lazarus, Mother!" Yehoshua squealed.
      All rushed out with flutes and drums
and raised a ruckus with their timpani.

Amid the surging confluence I saw
      the two boys waving and jumping for joy
before throwing themselves into each other.
      Everywhere someone attended someone.
Now, to hold that baby . . . But then the boy

and his "brother" Lazarus ran over to me.
      Before I could guess what they meant,
I was running and laughing, no older than ten,
      crowned The Maqqaba, Judas himself.
I commanded a mission. These brothers I sent,

Simon and Jonathan, would spy on the camp

      of Israel's enemies, all stirring their pots,

spreading blankets on their roofs . . . Treacherous.

      The honor of putting a frog in the sock

of old man Nicanor required we draw lots.

The voice of Miriam called us back to Nazareth.

      It was time to prepare for her husband's return

and all the other tired workmen of the town.

      A new order of festivity was now prepared.

There was something here for me to learn.

SPECTACULUM X

Sed et usque hodie ita praestatur a Domino.

Lazarus had earlier explained how they
   had mostly come to Nazareth to deal
as distributors of musical instruments.
   But now all conversation ceased.
While everyone worked, a singing, unreal,

emerged throughout the town, pulsing
   tones and lyrics haunting the stones:
"In you, O Lord, I take refuge . . .
   . . . my strength from my mother's womb."
I found a chore and prayed from my bones.

At the glory of twilight came the signal.
   Yehoshua eagerly signaled back,
and all assembled in quiet order,
   bedecked in flowers and fronds of palm.
But on first sight of the men, no lack

of vocal clamor ensued, the women's shrill
  trilling, the children shedding all calm.
Someone gave me an Egyptian sistrum
  to jangle my welcome, as beating drums
and tooting flutes coalesced in a single psalm.

And there was Yosef in the lead, dancing
  like David escorting the Holy Ark.
And as if on cue, repeated on each return,
  his son ran into his outstretched arms
to be lifted and carried in the growing dark.

SPECTACULUM XI

Venite, benedicti Patris mei.

To my surprise, the wedding of last night
      was to continue, so the evening meal
was another feast for bride and groom!
      How well I had learned the night before
the joy that comes from making real

angelic service to those whose love
      was freely woven by tradition's loom.
Yehoshua could read my thought, and looked
      into my eyes. "Your book," he said,
"is no less than this, a private room."

I wept, shamelessly, not knowing why.
      I trusted that the import would come clear.
He took me by the hand, again, and placed it
      in his mother's hand, who held me close
like that baby I had held before, so dear.

She sang to me, and spoke to me like one
      with nothing else to do, and I
began to see myself in clarity, as one
      more prone to end a thing than start
that which my fears persuade will die.

She told me that tomorrow I must go
      with Yosef and Yehoshua, to be
with them where they would walk each month
      to be alone with Abba, the Father.
I thanked her for her kindness, and agreed.

SPECTACULUM XII

Veni, vidi, credo.

The prophet Jeremiah was invoked that night.
   Over espoused heads, Yosef held his hands:
"See, I place my words in your mouth."
   I plucked kinnor, the Davidic harp,
as we sang, "*Gathered from foreign lands . . .*"

I did not oversleep the next morning's *todah*.
   Three hours was the hike to Mount Tabor
which loomed to the east. Another hour
   to climb it. But then the shock to learn,
they would carry my waterlogged door

without my help the entire way. No.
   I begged them, no. But it could not be.
Five hours, all told, they carried my wood
   to the mountain top, and there they prayed.
In my shame, all I wanted to do was flee.

The door was gaping, inviting escape.

    My heart was pounding. I must think.

Nothing about running would harmonize

    with the life I'd come to know in Nazareth.

I asked Yehoshua for water to drink.

On that pinnacle of Mount Tabor, I drank

    from my young friend's water skin.

We stood together before my door,

    in truth, my book, and we embraced.

Serene, I turned the page and passed within.

THE RED LAWN

1

Neither the swamp of bad sinuses nor

white-robed injunctions could come between

Sam and that test-pattern sky. His chore

began so long ago. How does one wean

someone of duty? The sketchy records in

Sam's medical history summary have been seen

as proof positive we can never win.

His cranium is labyrinthine misfiring mush.

At least he is victim of, not the worker of sin.

I closed his file and shouldered my bag in a rush.

The sky Sam peers into at each dusk and dawn,

the nebulae he nibbles as midnight toilets flush

we never see. By running stream, a fawn.

As if the promised return were any day

his mind stays parked on the red lawn.

Genesis 49, the eighteenth verse doth say,

I long, oh Lord, for your deliverance to flower.

On the head of *this* pin we should dance and play.

2

Not knowing the day nor even the hour

any more than Sam does, there I was, stalled

in traffic as that sky Sam loves began to shower.

On the turnpike shoulder I dialed and called

for rescue, having pushed my auto's weight

that Ephrem the Syriac terms "walled,"

by which the human body, though grave freight,

is the temple wall for the Holy Covenant's Ark.

The day was Friday, and the hour was late.

I sat in silence in the headlight-flashing dark.

Shuddering from passing trucks, my socks curled,

I twisted my key, but only made the engine bark.

Save the walled weight of the whole natural world

bending itself back into planetary mass,

no explanation occurred for my flag being furled.

Adam's curse did come to mind. Alas,

I must wait like a patient for the hospital meal,

like the pupil in his special education class.

3

Robbed of trajectory, the subject will feel

helpless. Just as space abhors a vacuum,

the mind abhors this feeling. It must make real

the most futile intention. See the brain bloom?

CT scans don't lie. Trapped here, you can see

I took myself to a diagnostic conference room.

Unlike the patient on the red lawn who is free

enough to be swallowed up by the black hole,

this evening's subject is normal. This one will flee

the extinction of purpose, assume a role

on a desert island or from inside an iron mask.

This one's past can have no claim on his soul.

Or so he thinks. Rebutting himself he dares to ask:

If persons in your past have no such claim,

then to what end the soul, what earthly task?

And here it seemed he was Jacob gone lame,

the red lawn's solitude his only meat.

Shall he propose a rose by a different name?

4

What pointless duty, this keeping one's seat?

Shouldn't this be the last Cumaean song

for the last age when our offspring cheat

the intruder, Death, who now has ruled so long,

whom Ambrose called the merciful remedy

to the wretchedness spawned by the first wrong?

Instead, wretchedness and wrong will be

our Lucina and Apollo praising their consul

while he carves and consumes us endlessly.

Behold the nodding world, behold the duel

between Nissan and the grappling hook of a truck

that tows away those thoughts, so cruel.

I was so quickly proud of all my luck!

The mind's diagnostic room was gone!

I was free again to pass the buck . . .

I dreamt that night of some swamp at dawn

and a windshield traced in descending curve.

Sam was still parked on the red lawn.

5

. . . a sliding near collision . . . What? Swerve!

Avoid Saturn's day, Israel's Shabbot.

Must I emerge pondering God's will to serve?

Origins and last words of final rest are my lot.

Today I am an "on call" worker, and so

the phone may ring, and I be majestically shot

into my own denial before the cock's crow.

"Welcome to the historical present," I say

to St. Mark, or anyone who may know

his use of Greek in that gospel where he'll play

with language at life's core. A feat this rare,

all that prolapse in tense that here forges a way

but eludes recognition, has its flair.

All this before my foot even touched the floor.

Go figure. He also serves who doesn't care.

And so began another day of the door,

the swinging wide, the passing through,

the knobs we twist and sometimes implore.

6

The face in the mirror's frame has no clue.

The feet on the bathroom tile cannot hide.

Exploding like piazza pigeons, everything flew

to anywhere known in sleep as scattered wide

only to settle back onto my cobbled brow

as the cooing untrue and the not quite died.

Example: *Saturday is code for a possessed sow.*

This was one of those false allegations in sleep.

They can align malignantly, but don't ask me how.

You can brush your teeth, but all you will keep

are these poisoned thoughts, the motley clothes

of the seven deadly virtues, too unfunny to weep:

respectability, childishness, timidity to your toes,

dullness, sentimentality, censoriousness, and worst

of all, that depression of spirits the genius knows.

How brilliant I could have been. What a thirst

for knowledge I once had. It was I who knew

before the research of the first cosmic burst!

7

That you may know that I am who

in sorting laundry, to name one chore,

is a genius, although with bleach, it's true,

I've Rorschached shirts in a single pour,

see me rise and walk onto my own red lawn.

Regular cycle. Normal soil. What a bore,

this dominion with the clean bones gone,

these spinning hollow limbs akimbo found

entangled, blind and sadly withdrawn.

But there it is, so soon, the frightening sound

of a crisis somewhere, signaled by my phone.

So soon, freed from my mundane round.

Sam's celestial spheres may now be shown

to round me with a different sleep. From my side

will there be plucked the bone of my bone?

A different washing was needed to turn this tide.

I had nurtured my share of seductive lies.

But now it was the call to care, not "I tried."

8

Neither the lamp that talent implies

nor academic laurels snugly framed

prepares us for the paroxysmal size

of choosing when it risks being blamed.

Nothing noble here. Less concern

for Sam than for myself being shamed.

This is my profession's sting, to learn

that Lord Jim's secret vice is mine

and then deftly avoid its persistent burn.

And so, as seeing the emergent sign

of Sam's collapse on his red lawn

curbed my initial impulse to whine,

my move was to simply play my pawn

and wait for fate to show me more,

to tip its hand until my queen is gone.

But a second thought rose from the very floor,

and I stopped in my tracks in mid pacing

until my groping mind could fathom it and not ignore:

9

The lambskin scroll of a Torah still

is judged by a child and not a man

for legibility when flawed by age, until . . .

Wait. Is that what strikes me, inspires this plan

in my brain? Angel! I translate your oblique tale:

"Sam's gaze upon you, not sky, is life's bread to man."

My own species of ruin is the fear I will fail,

Sam's is the failure to know normal fears.

But coherence is strangely evident, even in betrayal.

If I listen well I can hear the rousing cheers

of the red lawn's multitudes, made whole

and frolicking beyond these present tears.

Sam's eyes searching mine and not mine into his soul

is what drives me through the rain to his side, to undo

my own hollow, loveless acts of control,

hoping for Sam's childlike verdict reading into

my soul the star of Bethlehem, the songs of hope,

the word of three gifts, all clear and true.

STOOPED IN MY BRAIN'S AMYGDALA

STOOPED IN MY BRAIN'S AMYGDALA

Stooped in my brain's amygdala, synapse central,
Mr. Not Quite, crisis supervisor, rules. Gone,
the cortexian threat assessment. Absent, the search
for data, that give-and-take between world and mind.
Alone, that useless appendix commands all adrenals.

Mr. Not Quite assumes the worst and hits the switch.
The signal makes of all organs a single withering god.
Headshrinkers can't fathom amygdala, my bombing well.
Virgins have been sacrificed and books have been burned
by its remote-controlled surgical strikes. Gone,

the sublime duet, first amygdaline occupants.
Gone, their otherwise graceful flights that triggered
otherwise-aimed racing heart and respiration.
My amygdala must have been larger then, before
the brain's cortex migrated to the skull's suburbs.

And who should then move into my cranial core?
Quasimodo. Not Quite. The deaf hunchback himself.
But this isn't the pitiful version played by Charles Laughton,
leaning on a gargoyle, asking to be turned to stone.
This one must be channeling his evil master, the magistrate

who condemned Esméralda and her goat to the stake.
If he were to confine his meddling to pouring adrenaline
over the brain's parapets into the body's writhing muscles
for coping with saber-toothed tigers he'd be more useful.
But he now makes me the crisis. His method is diabolical.

He compels me to expeditions that put my soul at risk,
to trace the signs and vestiges of the lost Paradise.
His mission is to have me linger forever in neutral zones
to ponder the ruin of this world and feed on its carcass.
Mr. Not Quite assumes the worst and hits the switch.

I MUST HAVE MISSED THE MEMO

I must have missed the memo. Winter's last pitiful stinkbug
makes for the bathroom tile along the carpet and stops short.
A knock on the door is Pete, serving me the indictment of
Chronos. I am as stoic as my friend the stinkbug. The choir
will survive my morning dalliance with Madame *Kairos*.

Choirs are the great survivors. More than show biz, these
angelic legions, taking the cue from Bethlehem, endure
even the slaughter of innocence. She too is a survivor.
More like a hologram, she is here with me nonetheless.
I am buying a ticket from her through a window slot.

From inside her ticket booth she reigns in magnificence.
Her mercy is devoid of sentimentality. She packs smarts.
You heard me. Smarts is her trademark. But it takes me,
the misser of memos, to not be misled by the obvious.
The bug moved unseen and now clings to a vertical edge.

Why do I have this idea that she'd have the answer?
Go figure. A dozen roses by any other name would be
what? The answer to what? You're not making sense.
You'd be wise to rehearse the question she'd ask
that would warrant your fist of blossoms in her face.

I know! It is the permanence of the *kairosian* end,
that focus she has on the "uncaused cause," for example.
The answer to all the questions resides in permanence.
Even if you could take her away from all this boothness,
could you offer a tiny amygdala shared with Not Quite?

Walter Pidgeon on the Forbidden Planet, his own id
materialized and run amuck just to keep Anne Francis,
his daughter, from leaving him, would seem a paragon
compared to you getting your ticket punched by her
from inside your brain. Resume the stinkbug death march.

YOU'RE SUCH A ROMANTIC

You're such a romantic. That's why I like you. You'll never
make the grade of cynics who genuinely believe in the cause
of launching free will into outer space where it aimlessly
drifts while recording the void. You've figured out that no
history is made when the historians are all liquidated, when

thought crimes morph into kindness crimes, or aptness crimes,
or even trueness crimes. You'll sacrifice a Telstar's sleek
for the one true love. Given half a chance, you'll shamelessly
flaunt even the Constitution. You'd make your bitter pill not Cain's
but that of Jacob, Duchamp's bachelor peering into dreams,

before you'd ever be the bitch of anyone's Quasimodo.
You would be clothed in melancholy babies, each sublime.
Your solitude will ripen only in the tangled thatches of Church.
Only the last word in social context will satisfy your version
of free will, the romantic version. That's why I would bring you

coffee each morning, breakfast in bed if I could cook, or even
read *Wuthering Heights* to you from cover to cover. You'd love it.
That's how you know it's hopeless to run with the postmoderns.
Best bet is the doctrine of how it is. This question mark
grows like a Chia pet around "how it is," the world's first

Question-mark Doctrine. There will be war with the revisionists
who down through the ages seek to dilute it. You'd love that, too.
Here at last is a war worth fighting, to preserve the hairy truth
that "how it is" will never be merely empiricism or cynicism,
but rather the question lived to its logical conclusion. Joy.

I see that you want proof of that logical soundness. Sound.
The village idiot is pronouncing that word intensely in my ear.
A syllogism should suffice. If Bette Davis in *Now, Voyager*
is it, and Claude Rains is how, then Paul Henreid is more than is.
It's the "more than" that makes the proof for I AM WHAT AM.

I UNDERSTAND IF THIS LOGIC ESCAPES

I understand if this logic escapes full comprehension.
The sound that accompanies tongues of fire can obscure
perception of logical soundness. Thermopolis, Wyoming,
comes to mind. Sunk like negative film in a chemical dish,
it slowly emerges as the definitive print: of sight, for sight.

But more about that later. First we need to be treated
for our "cat scratch fever." Then we have to appreciate
the implications of the Big Bang and Einstein's revolution.
Finally, it takes an Aquinian "should" alive in the cranium
competing with Mr. Not Quite's positivistic tyranny.

Only then will the thermite ignite for sound welding.
Reason is not just the sum of surgery's dismemberments.
It is also the craft it takes to build the real edifice.
And the real must be the mother of real invention.
It should be the icon to which we burn our votive candles.

At Le Mans, Steve McQueen hauls caboose to a finish,
solitary in the cab but a choir boy in the pit, singing tenor
in the harmonized legend of *polis* without even meaning to.
This is how the force of gravity inherent in Church holds
at abeyance the dark matter ever pushing toward utter absence.

And string theories notwithstanding, or posits of alternate worlds,
the infinitely regressive contingency of all existing things
spells out the necessary posit of the famous Question-mark Doctrine
concluding how rumors of God's demise are much exaggerated.
One must dodge the amygdaline fury and its sophist hirelings

who will brave all contradictions to discredit these findings.
They're programmed to attack the messenger, linking one
with even homicidal crimes, all to fence off open range.
One must be nimble in retort and solemn in deeds, one's ear
to the ground straining for the hoofbeats of coming Thermopolis.

IT'S ONLY WHEN YOU CAN'T FIND THE LAST THREAD

It's only when you can't find the last thread that clarity
and mystery can occupy the same space at the same time.
This may not sound important, or may seem merely comical.
And you'd probably be right about both. I've staked my life
on an obsolete craft. Lucidity is both useless and quite funny.

I'm Sorrowful Jones in *Little Miss Marker*, instructing
Shirley Temple in bedtime prayers. Ridiculous consternation
becomes classic when I'm Gallahad on the charger Regret.
Now a sap, you can't find the last thread and panic sets in.
There is serious risk of laughing oneself sick. An accident

is what it is. That's what you tell yourself to even stand how
doom or redemption seems to hang in the balance. Fate.
Your instinct is to take it on the lam. But not Sorrowful Jones.
He stays put, humming a tune by Kurt Weil, looking
all Bogart and fingering his lucky bullets in one clammy hand.

Who would suspect that in his pocket calibrations are exact.
At the click of a mouse he can snatch facts or measure risk
by the standard deviation. Mr. Not Quite, his nemesis,
dangles the standard deduction while his other hand pulls plugs.
This is the dreaded pairing advertised, a Mothra and Godzilla.

I'm the explorer of the tundra between here and Thermopolis.
That is my claim to fame in this blizzard we claim to share.
My data is an inventory of regulations met and schedules set,
but includes profundities like: "Nothing comes from nothing."
Instructions read: "These facts could be hazardous to your health."

Hazards is the central theme of my report. The baseline is zero.
The project is much like counter terrorist analysis, dots
ever connected in an arctic disconnect with fundamentals.
Each hazard is a lock for which you actually have the key,
and you walk like an Egyptian, challenged into underworld.

SUDDEN ACCELERATION ISSUES

Sudden acceleration issues are catching up with verdicts.
That's the report I want to read. Human error leaves a trail,
spores containing undigested curses dotting the landscape,
but show me the evidence of gremlins inhabiting machines.
Acceleration is insulted by such guilt by association.

Acceleration doesn't need humans. It is a cosmic and a subatomic
virtue. It set the tone from the beginning of time, error free.
It animates the machine that is this memo with its excellence . . .
that is if we distinguish between speed and verbosity.
The Deposit of Faith has isolated the root of human error as a virus.

It made all the headlines. I'd say its name is Quasimodo.
This is why I lean toward mundane usefulness even while
centered on the uselessness of these heavy files I carry over
my shoulder every day, a bundle of rags that became my Star
that is Born, my crowning antidote to his hegemonic virulence.

This just in with the rolling thunder-snow: the private sector
has cleared their parking lots and driveways promptly, but
the municipalities have let us down. Public streets still languish
in the merciless drifts of "winter mix" and nature's caprice.
Brian may have something. If it's true that the Russians

have dug up a woolly mammoth, extant in the Pleistocene
epoch, and have sold the DNA to the Japanese for cloning,
then international diplomacy and world peace is secure,
and efficient snow removal of public streets pales in import.
Government shouldn't be expected to meet its obligations!

The saga of Born Star is a genuine antibody, Trilby in *Svengali*
comes to mind. You are her impresario and *ludus doctore*.
She is the silent embrace of obligation, invisibly marching
straight past the fourth wall and through our living rooms.
She is the first saving domino to fall. She's wheat in the wind.

MY CLOCK DIED

My clock died right around the time they fixed my starter.
The fact that speed has a limit in that possessed by light,
it turns out that time has a limit, a quantifiable minimum unit
and a maximum edge along which only God can see
the follicles growing on its rounded surface waving hosanna's.

My breaks are starting to slip and the radio's on the blink.
Sorrowful Jones thinks he can hear the rustle of time's surface
as it bends with the curve of space, a kind of midair mating
of duration and distance while I dodge potholes in Norristown.
He always gets the best assignments. I get to call the tow truck.

And so it has always been for such as I, no northern lights
to while away the nights, no phantom deer to feed from my hand,
no secret code to break lest civilization crumple like a box.
I talk with Sorrowful less frequently now, but his transmissions
persist. He is the man most likely broken by Madame Kairos.

His data is flawless. His interpretation is matchless. A marked man.
She prefers covert operations that have tangible democratic results.
She'd call it leadership. He, ever the king-maker, cannot lead.
If he leads, it is by his sheer pitifulness that the tribes somehow unite.
This is no Cochise waiting in ambush, living at altitude,

living and breeding among the ancestral rocks that tell tales.
She has put a contract out on him whose candor had cost lives.
Now Sorrowful is going to have to learn how to be Cochise,
this time on the lam for real, asphalt jungle and sudden
taxi rides to out of state, the usual *film noir,* if you please.

It won't take long for him to get cornered. His radio waves
leave doubt that what we read is not on an automatic loop.
Which means that he might already be dead, or held somewhere
enduring water-boarding and sensory deprivation, or may
be in God's own witness protection program called Church.

A MAN NEEDS TO BE JUDGED

A man needs to be judged by his cumulative record, and half
that record is off the record. Another proof, if you will,
that justice can only be achieved in the light of Him, who stands
outside of contingency and has intimate commerce with all
molecules and forces, all Aolian plucking of super strings,

all of the inner life of a man, beyond the man's own knowing.
The intimacy of permanence is the Question-mark Doctrine at
its core commitment to reality. A necessary, inescapable consequence
from reasoned deductions and bald facts takes one nowhere else.
Nothing we regard as being real could actually exist without Him.

Sorrowful Jones, for example. In one of his last communiques
he wrote how he remained loyal to Madame Kairos who
singlehandedly had put the Question-mark Doctrine on the map.
She marshaled the patriots of democracy at the critical hour.
She holds the key to the city of Thermopolis, our homeland.

He wrote that he imagines himself astride the charger Regret
even as he is hunted by both his Lady and Not Quite's blight.
He believed in the prevailing of justice. He had stripped pretense
and was sucking the water from cactus like an Apache. His
horizons were now bleak, but his research was nearly complete.

That we can conceptualize completion at all is a miracle.
It is "image and likeness" all over again, the tools of my trade,
the building of language into an edifice of intimate permanence.
The ambition to breathe life into the inanimate is an alchemy,
even when best intended, that runs the risk of Not Quite's net.

I owe Sorrowful for that little tip as well. For Shirley Temple
he had put down his racing forms and had picked up the Bible.
He had dedicated himself to tracking down all hazards to
holiness even as he rubbed shoulders with sophist degenerates
on the snowbound streets of Amygdaline Central elites.

HE AVOIDS SCATOLOGY

He avoids scatology, but he has to admit, he's best *ex-cathedra*.
Nature's chair makes popes of us all. And just so, his encyclicals
issue to us the profundities we choose to encyclopedize. It is
the perfect circle in the great chain of life for such as he.
It is the justice promised by Plato enfleshed, a mammoth revived.

Thermopolis could be a kind of Jurassic Park for prehistoric
notions of *logos* and such, great hulking philosophies
grazing placidly in the endless canopy, obsolete questions
winging clawlike wings above, virtue then dropping deposits
of wisdom on the surprised heads of tourists visiting the park.

Or, Thermopolis isn't really a place but a state of mind. Hate it.
I'm up to here with reverence for states of mind. Tracing thoughts
is the code Sorrowful lived by, his state of mind beside the point.
Forging expeditions was the ticket in those days. The mind
was our Solomon's mines, and we pillaged treasures routinely.

We were young, and the treasures wasted on us, but he
knew the value of ready-mades and life's random flotsam.
So he spent his share of the treasure on new expeditions
until he went broke. By then he was working undercover, posing
as a broken down loser living alone and hand to mouth.

It was the perfect disguise for someone who is on the lam.
He skated through checkpoints to get behind the lines,
and that was when they found out their mistake underestimating
Sorrowful Jones, maybe odd in his penchant for keeping junk,
but dangerous with his linguistic traps snapping his song and dance.

Enough about him. He was never invited to Thermopolis. But I
have received an invitation by the Chamber of Commerce there.
I will build a hospital there where I can carry on my research.
"We will fight them on the beaches," my Longest Day pulling up,
and with a wave I climb in and sail away beyond amygdala.

SUITE NO. 1
FOR VERTICAL TABLE IN G MAJOR

I. Prelude

I had an epiphany after our last conversation. It was as plain
as that chalked blessing over the door from last January sixth.
The lecture about cellist Pablo Casals was over. I had raced
to get Monday's trash cans on the curb, and when all was quiet,
all rooms of our beloved domicile in order, especially the kitchen,
I found myself in a familiar reverie. The world was again pristine.

Pristine is not perfect. Perfect is all hands seeing the Elephant
as the maestro performs on cognition's vertical table in G major.
No. When speaking of houses, pristine is the best it gets.
So there I was, once again in love with this house we both love,
and I wanted to tell you something. Your plan to help me.
It's a noble plan. It reminds me of so many noble plans I've had.

The epiphany was this. It is my nature, my need, to see it pristine.
But it's also my need to make life easier for those who rely on me.
I only wanted, however clumsily, to enlist you in the Order of Pristine.
Your plan would make the lives of our comrades more difficult,
which, as I've said, violates the second imperative of my life here.
Fear not for me. My vertical offerings, God willing, defy gravity.

II. Allemande

It began in Frankfurt with the dodge that clears thresholds backwards.
The Sputnik asteroid aimed for my head back then was "the hand."
So for me it was to be the stage, where a big hand could mean stardom
not seeing stars, where skill in ducking can come in handy. Risky?
What's the worst that can happen? Missing a cue. Forgetting a line.
When rejection is tempo largo, presto launching is a good gamble.

If you don't feel sorry for me yet, just wait. Not that those early years
never had off-stage joys. There was the leather pants hiking club.
There were fascinating, if loud and vulgar, midnight parental debates.
What about Latin conjugation and times tables interrogations?
Nothing better than that, standing for hours of insults and panic.
Best was Christmas Eve first communion. But it's not for children.

And I learned how to fly. I had only to stretch across the air at
chest level, and there I was floating along. The trick was finding
the chest level zone and then pushing off just right. I never did
get the hang of steering or landing without pain. But floating,
rising higher and higher over the Frankfurt rooftops, this alone
made my whole childhood worth it. That, and my sister Becky.

III. Courante

Becky once said that promises made in dreams are binding,
more so than when awake because you make them only to
yourself. The trick is remembering them in the first place.
Keeping them is therefore usually hopeless as a mystery story.
This could explain why I need all my strength to sleep well.
And why unknown tongues are best without the subtitles.

Somehow she is a presence in this Georgian mansion with me,
never more than on the afore-referenced Feast of Epiphany,
so jolly with the candied shoes, prancing Wise Men, and
wayward banter. And the swarming frolic about the knees:
Generation Z. What a partner, she, in the post-pageantry chore
of bringing the house back to its pristine rest in forgotten oaths.

Bedtime lights just so. Amnesia settles on the Morris Room.
Becky could remind the upholstery of their sacraments.
She did as much in that Cold War flat in West Germany.
She could decode enemy communiques or slip behind
the lines and plant the bugs or the bombs as called for
by mission headquarters chief, her brother, Son of CIA.

IV. Sarabande

A far cry from the colonial on Meeting House Lane where the
framed family tree featured Christopher Hussey, Nantucket
Quaker whaling captain. Our Great White was Vietnam
and high school saw the old man waving a dead arm while
pinned to its back. And it saw me fleeing to a DC treehouse
where I apprenticed to the knowing-good-and-evil serpent.

But the sorcery ended in Hong Kong, in a concrete faculty cell.
I'm ahead of myself. I've skipped over many stages, both of life
and the kind with footlights. And you could care less if this
confession in alleged verse really proved itself worthy verse
or true confession or, God help us, both. Compelling as
masterful origami, the point is fragile, elegant pointlessness.

Let's not forget those aforementioned noble plans to help.
Now *there* is a résumé to curl your socks. You think you're
bored now, wait until I've recited the litany of my noble plans
both before and after Hong Kong, although I admit that before
I was all sense and sensibility not results oriented. After,
the nobility of results reigned, pinning me to the Great White.

V. Menuett

So there it is, sandwiched between perfect and pristine: poise.
Unafraid of good posture and humble cheer, remembering all
that is needed for distributive grace, partaking of divine inclusion
and singular purity, vertical table becomes flesh juggling plates.
Having, since Hong Kong, seen the Elephant and labored in the
vineyard of pristine, poise glimmers on the lit candles of Ivy Hall.

How fitting that the dance instructor past mistress of this house
was raised by circus-people parents. Where is poise more vital
than under the Big Top, the most primal of performance stages?
Its virtues are what haunts us, though I tell the children who visit
that ghosts inhabit its rooms upstairs to keep them from wandering.
All tours must end with the third floor, basement off-limits, too.

Basement ghosts, of course, are the most dangerous. Their job
is to destroy your poise, to abolish all memory of it with an undertow
of unforgotten failures posing as the Oracle of Delphi. If you go
down there you might find a long box, open the lid, and see your
own dead eyes staring back. That usually deters the innocent
from launching unsupervised expeditions into fundamentals.

VI. Gigue

Resigned determination is the ticket. Or is it determined resignation?
Somewhere in there is what I mean by poise. Resigned to
permanence, determined to dance. The false poise of yesterday
was determination to forge permanence while resigned to dance.
Resigned to dance. Sounds more familiar than some yesterday.
The Lamb of God is determined to dance grounded in obedience.

The secret to stage performance is first planting your feet. Unless
you are representing a comic character worthy of ridicule.
In that case, wander as aimlessly around the stage as possible
and chatter with solipsistic vigor like Napoleon on St. Helena.
So they say. Fortunately for me, a comic figure can suddenly
emerge from aimlessness into grand avenging pristine purpose.

His groundedness in permanence erupts before the audience.
His commitment to the dance, to the vertical table's feast, slaps
like a pie in the face even amid his vaudevillian hijinks. You realize
this fool is none other than Pepe le Moko in a Casbah encounter
with the beautiful Parisienne, Gaby. A conversation inspired epiphany
becomes another all hands at Ivy Hall seeing the Elephant.

THE GARDEN OF THE MOON

(SONNETS TO THE BODY)

MORNING MIMOSA

I raise a toast to surgery's reprieve

and form a silent prayer this life will pass

with few ordeals up nature's sorry sleeve.

No Pythian portent bubbles in my glass . . .

This dawn had found me worried, past regret,

for you, my body, by abuses undeserved

considering all your faithfulness, and yet

I sit here in this bar with plans unswerved

to measure out to you some future pain.

Like Bloody Bess toward England's Catholic folk,

it's nature's sleeve I'll blame, not my insane

abuses of my body made a joke.

Today's reprieve is no less verdict now

of what I'll reap from what I here endow.

BAROQUE MYSTIQUE

A papyrus scroll unrolls before my eyes.

The legend of one Imhotep, prodigious heart

of ancient healing art. In glyphs, here lies

a chance for clues on how and where to start

the search for his elusive burial mound.

Bonaparte's stone slab is strewn about

in pieces like those broken Laws we found

at Sinai's feet, an army poised to rout

the body's ignorance, baroque mystique.

Long before he saved the Roman Church

from history's lance, she'd turned the other cheek

and found in fragment earth sweet heaven's search.

The mummy that I look for, long preserved,

if found will doubtless leave me quite unnerved.

SUPPLY AND DEMAND

A rhapsody in bloom has splashed the sky

while solo clarinet insinuates a plea.

The poet, earth, remembers not to try

to preach its poem, spring, but simply be.

The mercy that is merchandise arrays

itself across the fruited planes of man.

And there, mixed in with architecture's ways,

Goat Sammy, the apostle of the perfect plan.

"Twice blest," he murmurs. Spousal dignity.

What was it that you said the other day?

You begged me throw my shoulders back and see

each mortal pound of flesh as spirit's way.

"Let it be done . . . ," the second Eve had said,

as second Creation implodes, revealed as Bread.

SELF-SUBSTANTIAL FUEL

That Hopkins skylark caged inside our bone house

has no business with the soaring hawk

who reads the ground for prey, even the lone mouse,

even for me as I take this morning walk.

The babbling bird inside me soars as well

but wings itself on insubstantial breezes,

or currents more substantial than can tell

by lone mouse senses fretting for what pleases.

The famine where abundance lies is not

the body's fault, not body politic

nor coiling DNA that codes each jot

and tittle of conception's awesome trick.

It lies inside our bone house, in the cage

where self-substantial fuel is all the rage.

Tad Cornell

MEMENTO MORI

This waiting for her call-back has me hung

between the Four Last Things and passion's call

to arms, some Hamlet panting with one lung

and scratching heart-break lesions in a thrall.

Your hyperactive system *in munia* works

a seeming random pattern of defense

against an imagined hostile force that lurks

outside your surface organ, at our expense.

Gene-pool legions must be all arrayed

to save us from the Vandals, thought to flee

the bulwarks they command from Hades' shade,

the walls of skin-cell corpses, *momento mori*.

Like ultra violet rays, I crave her voice

and ponder Yorik's skull, the end of choice.

CROSSING THE HALYS

"Croesus, having crossed the Halys, will

destroy a great empire," spake the Delphic seer.

This Lydian king swallowed a bitter pill

when such advice, like texting, so unclear,

persuaded him to march on Persia's king.

He found the empire lost to be his own.

The oracle called World will also bring

to bear its messages on Body's throne,

our minds, without respect to Natural Law

where personhood in presence, real exchange,

has common trust in Truth from which to draw.

She asked me why text messaging seems strange.

A poem can be messaged text as well,

straight from the throat of Delphi's jaws to hell.

THE LOINS HE GIRDS

Don't be slothful when your tripod glows.

Apollo's limo ride can dazzle. Words

will fail you, battered by the raging flows.

That's when he had earned the loins he girds.

Resist disintegration by the gift

of insight. Bless it. This is sound advice

your grandma might impart. A chance lift

like this may come but once, but then entice

your static daydreams. *Gnothi sauton,*

and don't forget to motorize your tripod.

Seize the day? I'd say seize the wanton

millennia by a single pearl with a prophet's rod.

I'd say keep your grandma close, and keep

your wits when shocking gods put you to sleep.

THIS HOUSE THE ANGELS GUARD

Poised to rout the body's ignorance, He

has marshaled Michael's legions for the same

unlettered donkey that He rode to be

that clarion call reserved for birth. His Name.

Commandments and Rosetta Stone restored

as one omphalus stone, this donkey seats

himself on this earth's navel, gratefully adored

and eager to adore. I dine with Keats

and Shakespeare in this house the angels guard.

I'm more like braying Bottom than the colt

of pedigree that earns the title: Bard.

But angels shower me with favors. This dolt

has status never earned but by His Name.

His army's poised to rout the body's shame.

MOZART'S SEVENTEEN SONATAS

Deciphering such declamation needs

a Holy Ghost to make distinctions that

pertain to consequences sprung in deeds

and not the Mount Olympus habitat.

Decoding what the Pythia utters here

is calling for a good deal more than what

Apollo offers babbling omphalus cheer

that young and drunk Goat Sammy could, but

for access, cryptic luck and broadcast fear.

The scholars all agree the case is shut.

The action's with the conclave come to hear

and not with gods just sitting on their butt.

Mozart's seventeen sonatas, here.

Interpret that. Prepare to shed a tear.

HOW POLIS SEES

It's sculpture that explains how polis sees,

sings, or hears and dances till you crave

for touch, the taste that brings you to your knees,

the lover's fragrant smoke beside the grave.

The three dimension message has the best

of chances to survive what time has done

so far, more shapely than the hollow chest

decayed. Sculpture is no medium to shun.

But what is sculpture in itself, all posed

and pedestalled, here occupying space?

You'll know it not from models who had dozed

or men of research always on the chase.

The sculptor knows the dread of absent stone

to monument the world with life alone.

THE SHEPHERD'S SHAPE

You'll know it by imperviance to theme

that is not locked into The Holy Rock.

More than nascent form, like Peter's dream,

it's the shepherd's shape among the flock.

The only theme is faithfulness to Real

and Presence that is lovelorn rhyme

and reason, gymnast, making its appeal,

the marriage of eternity and time.

That sculpture should be known as something fast

may strain credulity unless you know

its rule is less for measure than for last

impassioned pleas to never have to go.

The cup we share in monumental theme

is bodily thrust into a dusty scheme.

AND YOU WALK ON AIR

And you walk on air like Fred Astaire

in love with New York's belle, you season's fool,

beyond all acrobatics, debonair,

you find yourself enrolled in her sweet school.

Some would say that honesty cannot

be found among the body's lexicon,

but Gnostic threads expose their cynic's lot

that Calvin staked his fated life upon.

Appearing on a wayside hill, she speaks

with rapid-fire sorrow for the loss

and all the promise that the body seeks.

She points with vigor toward a distant cross.

Just so, my New York belle appeared to me

and this man's body felt like one in three.

THE GARDEN OF THE MOON

That man was formed from dust is hardly more

astonishing than Universe from naught.

The garden of the moon where I implore

the woman's condescension can't be taught.

The roots of weeds shred out with sideways thrust

and piles of mulch, all in the Ignatian book.

But what surprises most is that I trust

my thumb, so lunar green, to bait the hook

that caught the fish that swallowed Caesar's coin.

The garden of the moon is utter gift

like heart to heart and spousal loin to loin

or sighting land when all you had was drift.

The woman that is birthed from out my chest

is teaching me from lessons with one test.

LEGEND'S TEXT

Aquinas ended life with only straw

as limit of self knowledge in this world

according to his last words that I gnaw

upon. Goat Sammy with his flag unfurled

is claiming that he knows what happened next.

The straw, he says, turned into river reeds,

another Syrinx become a legend's text,

a sigh of loss become the song he needs.

The maxim of The Seven Sages, "Know

Thyself," the boast of ancient wisdom carved

on Apollo's temple wall: fast food to go

for modern folks nutritionally starved.

"By Whom is each man known?" should be inscribed

where Seven Sages knew themselves and died.

MILVIAN BRIDGE

My tripod is at least now five stories high,

but won't move off an inch from omphalus dime.

So, I see backwards needing not to try

but actually be at Milvian Bridge, that time

when Roman shields bore emblems: Christ the Lord.

This history's crossroads, fateful battlefield,

is played out documentary style, a sword

as heaven-sent as Krishna art, but sealed

in heaven's own quite actual, pivotal sweep.

Benefactors welcome. Dedications proud

are all we need to get a good night's sleep.

But chivalry was born that day, the loud

announcement God's own Hollywood sense of art.

And passion's holy violence finds its part.

THE PRIZE OF HEMLOCK

The prize of hemlock waits for one who asks

the better questions than has answers prime.

"The polis leans toward just rewards for tasks

when every organ gives its all through time."

This was how I answered their foul cup.

I'd stamped it best I could indelible

on all their walls, with arrows pointing up,

which means the poison, quite incredible,

is just because I gave it all I had.

No point in arguing with time. To be

remembered living here, a place so sad

and joyful, knowing that my mind is free . . .

Last words seem pointless, but a prayer will steer

the conversation to "Hello, my dear."

CAUGHT A WHIFF

And Aesop thrown off Hyampeia cliff!

How generous the polis is to man.

But this researcher finally caught a whiff

of Imhotep, the doc who says he can.

The time for diagnosis is at hand.

The mummy stinks of moonshine, and is shy

to go on record with your case. The land

you seek is not this rotting under sky,

but polis of an ideal kind, unique

and throbbing like a garden in the moon.

So, I bequeath you, body, to the peak

where all the angels sing the mighty tune

that sculpts the painted poem in a dance.

That day has naught to do with fickle chance.

ABOUT THE AUTHOR

Tad Cornell (T. H. Cornell) spent his childhood until age twelve in Germany where his father worked for the US State Department (in actuality he was an agent in the CIA, as Cornell later learned). As a child actor in Germany, Tad appeared in a number of productions at the Frankfurt Playhouse, and starred each Christmas season in the Gian Carlo Menotti opera, *Amahl and the Night Visitors*.

His inter-spiritual explorations have taken him to Hong Kong, where he taught English in a Chinese middle school; a Trappist monastery in upstate New York, where he lived as a novice monk; Rome, where he studied theology at the Pontifical University of St. Thomas Aquinas (*Angelicum*); the streets of Manhattan and Houston, on behalf of charities advocating for homeless youth; and to his home base in Philadelphia, where he retired after several decades of teaching and directing social service programs for developmentally disabled adults.

He has a BA in English from Temple University, a master's degree in special education from Antioch College, and a master's degree in English literature from Villanova University. Cornell's former wife, author Marly Cornell, wrote *The Able Life of Cody Jane: Still Celebrating* about the life of their daughter.

Tad Cornell has essentially been an underground poet since producing his first book, *Glance Over at These Creatures* in 1977. Some of his poetry has been published conventionally; but much more of his work has been personally bound and hand-gifted, or presented in the form of poetry slams and avant garde stage productions (in Hong Kong, Houston, and Philadelphia areas), or on guitar and vocals as part of poetry/music fusion rock band, Edgar Allen and the Poettes, and other poetry performance ensembles.

Tad Cornell lives currently in Ivy Hall, headquarters of the International Institute for Culture, a Catholic study center in Philadelphia.

Also by Tad Cornell

Glance Over At These Creatures (Resources for Human Development, 1977)

Honey From the Rock & Hong Kong Elegies (Latitudes Press, 1988)

The Unspeakable Mating (Latitudes Press, 1989)

Chapbooks

Looking the Moon in the Face (1977)

Hollywood Diamond Exchange (1977)

Marco Polo (1977)

The Unspeakable Mating (1977)

The Promise of Silence (1978)

Rosie Knuckles Knows (1978)

Cough Poems for the Tickle (1978)

Hong Kong Elegies (1980)

Honey From the Rock (1985)

It Seems Important (1988)

Mine Umbra: Collected Poems 1985–1992 (1992)

A Single Pearl (1992)

Magnetosphere (1993)

Gloria Über Alles, dramatic adaptation of *Magnetosphere* with Stan Heleva (1994)

Svengali: The Musical (script and score, 1999)

Puzzle Me Back (2004)

Waving and Heaving (Poiein Anaphoran) (2005)

Sex and Melancholy (2005)

The Graphics of the Mouth (2006)

Spectaculum (2007)

The Red Lawn (2009)

Stooped in my Brain's Amygdala (2011)

The Garden of the Moon (Sonnets to the Body) (2014)

www.ingramcontent.com/pod-product-compliance
Lightning Source LLC
Chambersburg PA
CBHW032106080426
42733CB00006B/436